YANKEES AND REBELS

Stories of U.S. Civil War Leaders

BY STEVEN OTFINOSKI

Consultant:
Lyde Cullen Sizer, PhD
Professor of U.S. Cultural and Intellectual History
Sarah Lawrence College
Bronxville, New York

CAPSTONE PRESS
a capstone imprint

Connect is published by Capstone Press,
1710 Roe Crest Drive, North Mankato, Minnesota 56003
www.capstonepub.com

Library of Congress Cataloging-in-Publication Data
Otfinoski, Steven.
  Yankees and Rebels : stories of U.S. Civil War leaders / by Steven Otfinoski.
    pages cm.—(Connect. The Civil War)
  Summary: "Powerful leaders emerged during the victories and defeats of the Civil
War. Meet the people who planned the battles, led the attacks, and shaped the war
between the Yankees and the Rebels. Perfect for Common Core studies on analyzing
multiple accounts of an event"—Provided by publisher.
  Includes bibliographical references and index.
  ISBN 978-1-4914-2008-9 (library binding)
  ISBN 978-1-4914-2161-1 (paperback)
  ISBN 978-1-4914-2167-3 (ebook pdf)
  1. United States—History—Civil War, 1861–1865—Biography—Juvenile literature. I.
Title.
  E467.O85 2015
  973.7—dc23   2014023655

Editorial Credits
Adrian Vigliano, editor; Veronica Scott, designer; Wanda Winch, media researcher;
Kathy McColley, production specialist

Photo Credits
(20th ME & 15th AL) by Dale Gallon, Courtesy of Gallon Historical Art, www.gallon.
com, 39; Bridgeman Images/Chicago History Museum, USA, 29 (bottom); Capstone,
25; Corbis: Bettman: 4; Courtesy of HarpWeek, LLC, 19; CriaImages.com/Jay Robert
Nash Collection, 31, 32, 35, 37; Library of Congress: Prints and Photographs Division,
6, 7, 9–18, 20–24, 26–28, 30, 33, 36, 38, 40–45; Shutterstock: Ekaterina Romanova,
ornate frames, Ensuper, cover (grunge colors), Extezy (vintage calligraphic elements),
f-f-f-f (old calligraphic décor elements), GarryKillan (damask ornamental designs),
Lucy Baldwin, rust abstract design, nikoniano, grunge stripe design, wacomka,
vintage floral background); Thinkstock: Stockbyte, 5; Wikipedia: Smithsonian
National Portrait Gallery, 29 (top); www.historicalimagebank.com Painting by
Don Troiani, cover, 34

Printed in the United States of America in Stevens Point, Wisconsin.
092014   008479WZS15

TABLE OF CONTENTS

CAUSES OF THE CIVIL WAR

As the United States grew in the 1800s, trouble developed among the states. Northern states were changing from a farming **economy** into one built on finance and industry. By 1804 all Northern states had abolished slavery, beginning a long process of freeing Northern slaves. Some Northerners felt slavery was morally wrong. But Southern **plantations** continued to rely on slave labor to farm crops such as cotton, sugar, and tobacco.

Harvesting crops such as cotton was brutal work. Plantation owners sometimes forced their slaves to work up to 15 hours per day.

Slavery was part of a larger divide between North and South. The two sides argued over states' rights. Southern states didn't want Congress and the president telling them what to do about slavery.

At this time new states were entering the Union. Lawmakers tried to keep a balance between new "slave states" and new "free states." Politicians tried to satisfy both sides with the Compromise of 1850. This act allowed California to enter the Union as a free state. It also allowed voters to decide for or against slavery in the territories of Utah and New Mexico. To further satisfy the South, Congress passed a new Fugitive Slave Act. This act made it illegal to interfere with the returning of runaway slaves to their owners. Northerners who opposed slavery were furious about this act.

economy—the ways in which a country handles its money and resources

plantation—a large farm found in warm areas

Violence Erupts

Problems continued with the Kansas-Nebraska Act of 1854. This act allowed residents of the two new territories to vote on allowing slavery. Nebraska's residents voted to be a free state. In Kansas people were sharply divided on the issue. Violence between the two groups earned the territory the nickname "Bleeding Kansas." The situation made Northerners so angry they formed the Republican Party. This new political party opposed slavery from spreading to new states and territories.

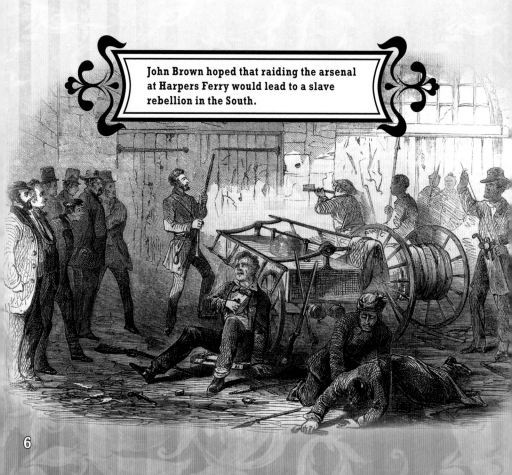

John Brown hoped that raiding the arsenal at Harpers Ferry would lead to a slave rebellion in the South.

John Brown

John Brown, a radical **abolitionist**, first gained attention during the 1854 violence in Kansas. He and his group killed five pro-slavery settlers. In 1859 he led a raid on Harpers Ferry, Virginia. Brown planned to take weapons from a federal **arsenal** and arm slaves. He wanted the slaves to start a rebellion in the South. But the plan failed and Brown was tried and hanged. Southerners saw Brown as a villain. To Northerners who opposed slavery, he was a hero.

Democrats ran against Republicans in the presidential election of 1860. The divide between North and South was sharper than ever before. Some Southern leaders said that their states would **secede** if the Republican candidate, Abraham Lincoln, was elected. On November 6, 1860, Lincoln won the election.

abolitionist—a person who called for the immediate end of slavery before the Civil War
arsenal—a place where weapons are stored
secede—to formally withdraw from a group or an organization, often to form another organization

POLITICAL LEADERS OF THE UNION

Both sides in the Civil War (1861–1865) had strong political leaders. Political leaders provided the soldiers and money to fight the Civil War. They also tried to keep up the spirits of the public with speeches and writings.

Abraham Lincoln

1809–1865

Abraham Lincoln was the first president to face a war that threatened to tear apart the United States. Lincoln wanted to keep slavery in the Southern states where it already existed. He did not want it to spread to new territories and states. Lincoln thought slavery would eventually disappear as industry replaced the plantations where slave labor was most needed.

But Southern leaders didn't trust Lincoln. On December 20, 1860, just 44 days after Lincoln's election, South Carolina seceded from the Union. By the time Lincoln was **inaugurated** president in March 1861, six more Southern states had seceded. These and four more states would later form the Confederate States of America. Lincoln continued to say he didn't want to end slavery altogether. This stand allowed him to keep the border slave states of Kentucky, Missouri, Delaware, and Maryland in the Union.

Southerners did not trust Lincoln. Many feared he would use presidential power to end slavery.

inaugurate—to swear an official into public office with a formal ceremony

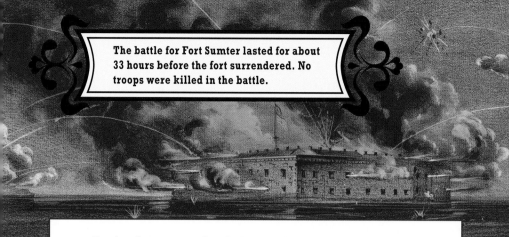

The battle for Fort Sumter lasted for about 33 hours before the fort surrendered. No troops were killed in the battle.

On April 12, 1861 Confederates fired on the Union's Fort Sumter in South Carolina. The Civil War had begun. Lincoln called for 75,000 men to serve in the Union army. The South was a stronger enemy than many Northerners had expected.

Eventually Lincoln changed his position on slavery. On January 1, 1863, he released the Emancipation Proclamation. It ordered the end of slavery in the Confederate states. Lincoln was careful not to end slavery in the border states because he needed their support. Southerners refused to follow Lincoln's orders. But the Emancipation Proclamation gave the North a strong new focus of fighting to end slavery.

Many Northerners grew tired of the war. They wanted a compromise with the South. Lincoln refused. He wanted to keep the Union whole. As the presidential election of 1864 drew closer, Lincoln's popularity faded. But then the Union won several important battles. The tide turned in the North's favor, and Lincoln easily won a second term. A month after Lincoln's second inauguration, Confederate General Robert E. Lee surrendered. The North had won the war.

On April 14, 1865, Lincoln was shot by Confederate sympathizer John Wilkes Booth. The president died the next morning.

Abraham Lincoln delivered his second inaugural address on March 4, 1865.

"Now we are engaged in a great civil war, testing whether that nation, or any nation so conceived, and so dedicated, can long endure. We are met on a great battle field of that war. We have come to dedicate a portion of it, as a final resting place for those who died here that the nation might live."

— Abraham Lincoln, the Gettysburg Address, November 19, 1863

Edwin Stanton

1814–1869

Lincoln surprised many when he appointed Edwin Stanton as secretary of war. Stanton was a Democrat who had opposed Lincoln's presidential campaign.

Stanton proved to be a good choice. He reorganized and strengthened the War Department. He worked to end **graft** and corruption. He put railroads under military control to help move supplies and soldiers. After Lincoln was assassinated, Stanton stayed on to serve President Andrew Johnson.

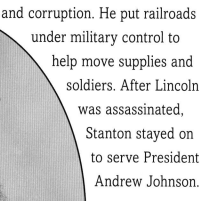

Harriet Beecher Stowe

1811–1896

Abolitionist Harriet Beecher Stowe played an important role in the fight against slavery. Upset by the Fugitive Slave Act of 1850, Stowe showed the cruelty of slavery in her book, *Uncle Tom's Cabin*. Published in 1852, the book sold 300,000 copies in its first year. Many Americans saw the horrors of slavery for the first time. During the Civil War, Stowe visited the White House. President Lincoln is said to have greeted her with these words: "So you're the little woman who wrote the book that made this great war."

Fact

Stanton opposed President Johnson's policies to help Southern states rebuild after the war. When Johnson tried to remove Stanton from his cabinet, Stanton blocked himself in his office and refused to leave. He later led the movement to impeach Johnson.

graft—illegal practice such as bribery used to secure gains in politics or business
impeach—to bring formal charges against a public official who may have committed a crime while in office

13

William Seward

Abolitionist William Seward twice failed to gain the Republican presidential nomination. Lincoln made his former rival secretary of state. During the war some European nations, such as England, sympathized with the Confederates. Seward helped convince these nations not to aid the South. He later served as secretary of state for President Johnson.

Frederick Douglass

1818–1895

After escaping slavery around age 20, Frederick Bailey changed his last name to Douglass. In 1841 he gave a speech about slavery to the Massachusetts Anti-Slaverly Society. The group hired him to speak on the subject. Later Douglass started the abolitionist newspaper the *North Star*. During the Civil War he met several times with President Lincoln to discuss the slavery issue. Douglass also helped recruit soldiers for the first all-black Union regiments. After the war Douglass continued to fight for the rights of black Americans and women.

Salmon P. Chase

1808–1873

Senator Salmon Chase was not an abolitionist, but he opposed the spread of slavery to new territories. He ran against Lincoln for the Republican presidential nomination and lost. Lincoln named him secretary of the treasury. Chase raised money for the Union's war effort. He also helped create a national banking system that is still used today. Later, as chief justice of the United States Supreme Court, Chase oversaw Andrew Johnson's impeachment trial.

Salmon P. Chase

POLITICAL LEADERS OF THE CONFEDERACY

Jefferson Davis was inaugurated president of the Confederate States of America on February 18, 1861.

Jefferson Davis

1808–1889

Jefferson Davis knew war before he became president of the Confederacy. He served in the army in the Mexican War (1846–1848). He later became U.S. senator for Mississippi. As senator he supported slavery and states' rights. He went on to become secretary of war under President Franklin Pierce. Davis returned to the Senate in 1857 but resigned his seat when the Southern states began to secede. Davis wanted to be named commander in chief of the Confederate army. Instead he was elected president of the Confederacy.

President Davis was not as strong a leader as President Lincoln. A hot temper, poor health, and weak planning skills hurt his ability to lead. At first Davis was popular with Southerners for his support of the Confederate cause. He became less popular as the war dragged on and the Confederates began losing more battles.

On April 2, 1865, Union troops closed in on the Confederate capital of Richmond, Virginia. Davis fled but was captured in Georgia on May 10, 1865. He was charged with treason but never convicted.

Fact

Jefferson Davis' birthday is a legal holiday in three Southern states.

Alexander Stephens

1812–1883

Alexander Stephens served as a member of the House of Representatives from his home state of Georgia. Stephens argued against secession before the war. But when Georgia voted for secession, Stephens remained faithful to his state. He was elected vice president of the Confederacy in February 1861. He was often at odds with President Davis, and soon began arguing for a peaceful end to the war. He even negotiated with Union General William Sherman about Georgia making a separate peace with the Union.

In February 1865 Stephens led a **delegation** to the Hampton Roads Conference. His group wanted a peace agreement with the North to end the war. President Lincoln was there. The conference failed because the two sides couldn't agree on issues such as slavery. Two months later the North won the war. Stephens was arrested and spent about five months in prison.

delegation—a group that speaks for a country

The political magazine *Harper's Weekly* published a cartoon showing Stephens meeting Lincoln at the Hampton Roads Conference. The meeting lasted only four hours.

MILITARY LEADERS OF THE NORTH

Many Civil War military leaders were professional soldiers, trained at the the United States Military Academy at West Point. Others were businessmen or politicians. Both North and South had skilled commanders who directed the course of the war.

George McClellan

1826–1885

General McClellan was nicknamed "Young Napoleon of the West," because, like the French leader, he was a great military organizer. This skill led President Lincoln to make McClellan general of all Union forces in November 1861.

McClellan turned the Union's volunteers into a disciplined fighting force. But when the time came to fight, he was slow to move against the enemy. Lincoln replaced McClellan with other generals three times because of this failing.

Lincoln met with McClellan after the Battle of Antietam. McClellan ignored the president's urging to march after Lee.

McClellan led the Union to an important but costly victory at the Battle of Antietam in September 1862. It was the bloodiest day of the Civil War. About 23,100 soldiers were killed, wounded, or went missing. McClellan did not chase the beaten Confederate army south. Lincoln saw McClellan's hesitation to follow the Southern army and finish it off as a serious problem. He relieved McClellan of command for the last time, ending the general's military career.

McClellan became a strong critic of Lincoln's war policy. He argued for compromise with the South. Popular with many people, he was nominated for president by the Democratic Party in 1864. But Northern victories on the battlefield helped Lincoln beat him in the election.

Ulysses S. Grant

1822–1885

Grant quickly gained attention as a determined Union leader. His early victories are considered some of the most important Union successes.

Ulysses Grant failed at every job he tried, except for being a soldier. He did that so well he ended up the Union's leading general. Grant had been out of the military for years when he rejoined at the start of the war. Lincoln made him brigadier general. Despite showing bravery in his early battles, he suffered great losses at the Battle of Shiloh in Tennessee. Critics called for the president to replace him, saying Grant had sacrificed his men. "I can't spare this man." Lincoln replied, "He fights."

Harriet Tubman

1820-1913

Harriet Tubman escaped slavery in 1849. She is best known for leading more than 300 other slaves to freedom in the 1850s. During the Civil War she worked for the Union as a cook and hospital nurse. She also became a Union spy and served as a scout for raiding parties. On June 1, 1863, Tubman guided black Union soldiers on the Combahee River Raid in South Carolina. During the raid her group freed more than 700 slaves from nearby plantations.

General Grant continued to impress Lincoln. He won stunning victories at Vicksburg, Mississippi, and Chattanooga, Tennessee, in the summer of 1863. A stubborn warrior, he earned the nickname "Unconditional Surrender" Grant.

Grant's important victory at the Battle of Chattanooga forced the Confederate army to retreat into Georgia.

The Battle of Chattanooga 1863.

In March 1864 Lincoln put Grant in command of all Union forces. Grant's troops continued to clash with General Robert E. Lee's Confederate army across Virginia. Lee holed up in Petersburg and Grant laid **siege** to the city. Lee finally fled west and surrendered to Grant at Appomattox Court House on April 9, 1865. The two men showed great respect for each other. Grant was gracious in victory. He allowed the Confederate soldiers to keep their horses for use in spring planting when they returned home. Grant returned to Washington a hero. Greater honors would later come to him, including the presidency itself.

GRANT'S VIRGINIA CAMPAIGN

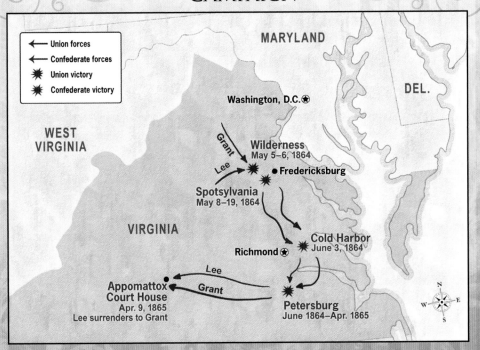

siege—an attack on a castle, fort, or other enclosed location

William T. Sherman

1820–1891

General Sherman's attack on Atlanta, Georgia, began in the middle of July 1864. On September 2 his troops captured the city. When Sherman's army left Atlanta in November, they destroyed much of the city.

After leaving Atlanta Sherman led his 62,000 troops on the "March to the Sea" across the state of Georgia. Moving eastward to the Atlantic coast, Sherman's goal was to destroy everything of military value in the Union's path. His troops destroyed farms, factories, and railroads. By taking away the Confederate army's supplies, Sherman hoped to end the war.

Sherman's troops wanted to destroy any resources that the Confederates could use.

Sherman arrived in Savannah on the Georgia coast on December 21. He sent a message to Lincoln, offering the city to the president as a Christmas present. Soon after, Sherman headed north into the Carolinas. He reached Raleigh, North Carolina, when news arrived that Lee had surrendered to Grant in Virginia.

Sherman did not believe that war was glorious and heroic. He once said "war is hell." He destroyed the South's economy to bring the war to an end.

Disabling railroad tracks was one way Sherman's troops could disrupt Confederate supply lines.

Philip Sheridan

1831–1888

General Sheridan led daring raids into Confederate territory. He became **quartermaster** general early in the war, providing troops with supplies. In early 1862 he became a colonel of the Second Michigan Cavalry. He led his men to victory at Booneville, Mississippi, which earned him the rank of brigadier general. Grant gave him command of the cavalry of the huge Army of the Potomac, stationed just outside Washington, D.C.

In August 1864 Grant appointed Sheridan commander of the Army of the Shenandoah Valley in Virginia. He was ordered to destroy enemy supplies and drive out Confederate troops.

In 1864, Sheridan (seated, center) led the Shenandoah Valley Campaign, which destroyed much of the South's food supply.

quartermaster—military department or officer in charge of getting supplies to troops

Martin Delany and the Black Union Soldiers

Martin Delany was one of the first blacks to attend Harvard Medical School. Before the war he spent several years helping Frederick Douglass publish his abolitionist newspaper the *North Star*.

After Lincoln's Emancipation Proclamation, the Union began recruiting free black men as soldiers. They served in segregated units commanded by white officers. There were no black Union officers until February 26, 1865, when Delany was given the rank of major. Delany was never given a field command, but he recruited many blacks to serve in the Union army.

By the war's end about 180,000 black men had served in the Union army. Black soldiers made up about 10 percent of the total number of Union army soldiers.

MILITARY LEADERS OF THE SOUTH

Robert E. Lee

1807–1870

Robert E. Lee remains one of the most respected Southerners in American history. His ability as a military leader was second only to his strong character.

Lee opposed secession from the Union. He didn't believe in slavery as an institution and freed some of his own slaves before the war. As war looked likely President Lincoln offered Lee the command of the Union army in Virginia. Lee rejected the offer and returned to his home state of Virginia when it seceded. Home and family led him to join the Confederate cause.

Lee was put in command of the Army of Northern Virginia in 1862. For the next three years he kept Southern hopes alive with his victories. One of his greatest was at the Battle of Chancellorsville in May 1863. Two months later he met defeat in the three-day-long Battle of Gettysburg. Lee escaped and headed south with his army.

The Union force at the Battle of Chancellorsville was almost twice as large as Lee's army, but the Confederates still managed to win.

General Lee later fought head to head with Grant in a series of battles known as the Overland Campaign. Overwhelmed by Grant's greater number of troops, Lee took a stand at Petersburg, Virginia. Lee held off the Union army for more than nine months before withdrawing.

Grant and Lee met again at Appomattox Court House in Virginia. The Southern general surrendered there on April 9, 1865. Lee was **paroled** on the day of his surrender.

After the war many people wanted Confederate leaders to be tried for treason. But Grant insisted that Lee not be put on trial.

parole—release from prison after serving less than the original sentence

The Mexican War—Training Ground for the Civil War

Robert E. Lee and other Civil War military leaders got their training in the Mexican War. Lee, then a young army officer, was sent to Texas. He worked as an army engineer building bridges crossing from Texas into Mexico. He soon proved a skilled soldier as well. He fought in the Siege of Veracruz and later in the invasion of Mexico City. General Winfield Scott, commander in chief in the war, called Lee "the greatest military genius in America."

Jefferson Davis commanded a unit called the Mississippi Rifles. Ulysses Grant, a lieutenant, was noted for skill and bravery.

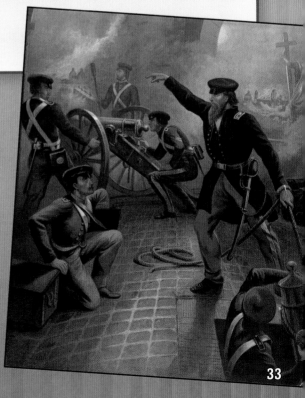

Ulysses Grant (standing, right) was part of the fight to capture Mexico City.

Thomas "Stonewall" Jackson

1824–1863

General Stonewall Jackson was a great strategist and a bold fighter. He earned his nickname at the First Battle of Bull Run in July 1861. Jackson stood bravely facing the Union attack. "There is Jackson standing like a stone wall!" Confederate General Bernard Bee is said to have told his men.

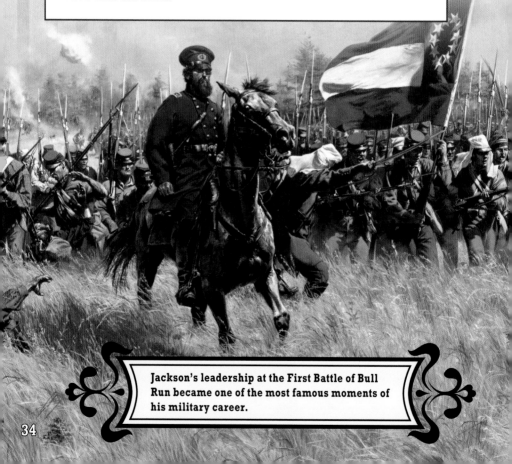

Jackson's leadership at the First Battle of Bull Run became one of the most famous moments of his military career.

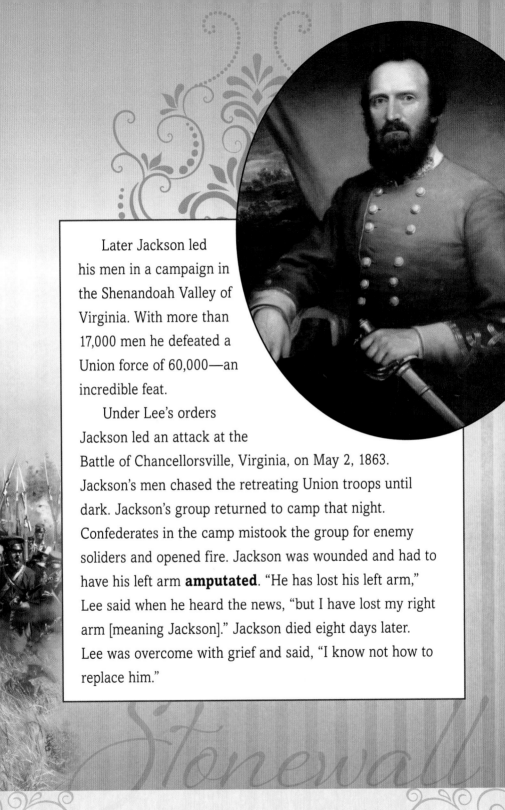

Later Jackson led his men in a campaign in the Shenandoah Valley of Virginia. With more than 17,000 men he defeated a Union force of 60,000—an incredible feat.

Under Lee's orders Jackson led an attack at the Battle of Chancellorsville, Virginia, on May 2, 1863. Jackson's men chased the retreating Union troops until dark. Jackson's group returned to camp that night. Confederates in the camp mistook the group for enemy soliders and opened fire. Jackson was wounded and had to have his left arm **amputated**. "He has lost his left arm," Lee said when he heard the news, "but I have lost my right arm [meaning Jackson]." Jackson died eight days later. Lee was overcome with grief and said, "I know not how to replace him."

amputate—to cut off someone's arm, leg, or other body part, usually because the part is damaged

James Ewel Brown "Jeb" Stuart

1833–1864

A skilled gatherer of war intelligence, Jeb Stuart was known as "the eyes of the army." In a raid on a Union camp, Stuart found war plans from Union General John Pope. Lee used these papers to help him win the Second Battle of Bull Run.

Stuart was also a daring calvary officer. In 1862 he boldly led his calvary in a huge circle around McClellan's army. He became famous for circling McClellan, but the Battle of Gettysburg brought trouble for Stuart. His cavalry arrived a day late to the battle. They had been riding south of Gettysburg on a raid. Stuart claimed that he misread his orders to stay near Lee and Gettysburg. Some believed he had made an honest mistake. Many others blamed him for the loss at Gettysburg and even the war.

When Jackson died Stuart took over his command temporarily. Stuart was wounded while fighting Sheridan's troops at Yellow Tavern, Virginia, outside Richmond on May 11, 1864. He died the next day. His death was another serious loss for the Confederates.

Stuart was killed by a Union sharpshooter whose unit was retreating from Stuart's cavalry.

James Longstreet

1821–1904

Lee called General Longstreet his "Old War Horse." At Gettysburg, Longstreet was in command of the Confederates' right wing. He was accused of delaying the order to attack and many blamed him for this major Southern defeat. Despite these accusations, Lee never blamed Longstreet and took the responsibility on himself. Many historians agree that Longstreet was unfairly accused of delaying his attack.

Longstreet went on to fight at the battle of Chattanooga in Tennessee. He also fought in the Wilderness Campaign of 1864, where he was seriously wounded.

At Gettysburg, Longstreet (center) advised Lee against the attack known as "Pickett's Charge." The attack failed, as Longstreet predicted.

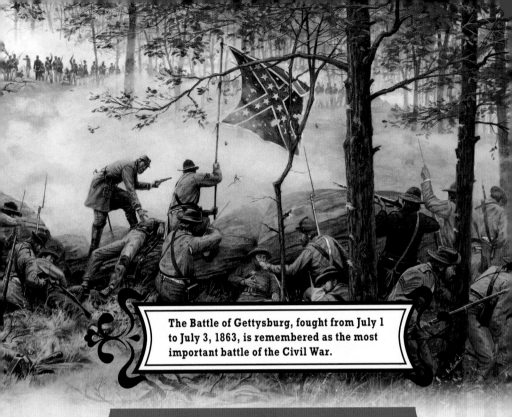

The Battle of Gettysburg, fought from July 1 to July 3, 1863, is remembered as the most important battle of the Civil War.

Sally Tompkins

1833–1916

When President Davis asked civilians to help treat wounded Confederate soldiers, Sally Tompkins acted. She paid to set up a hospital in a house in Richmond, Virginia. Her hospital quickly became the most successful in the South. When a new regulation required hospitals to be run by the military, Davis appointed Tompkins a captain of the cavalry. Her hospital treated 1,333 Confederate soldiers during the war and recorded only 73 deaths. After the war she continued to help veterans. Tompkins was buried with full military honors when she died at age 82.

BINDING THE NATION'S WOUNDS

The Civil War had great consequences for both the North, the South, and the nation as a whole. The loss of life was the worst of any war America had fought. The total death toll is estimated to be at least 620,000. The financial losses for both the North and the South were enormous.

Lincoln promised to deal fairly with the South. But radical Republicans in Congress wanted to punish the South. They wanted to protect the rights of freed slaves and hoped they would become Republican voters. Five days after Lee's surrender, Lincoln was assassinated.

John Wilkes Booth shot Lincoln while the president watched a play at Ford's Theatre in Washington, D.C.

Andrew Johnson, a Southerner, became president after Lincoln's death. He supported lenient policies toward the former Confederate states. In reponse, Republican leaders called for his impeachment. Johnson was impeached by the U.S. House of Representatives. He avoided conviction by one vote, but his power as president was seriously damaged.

Taking effect on December 6, 1865, the Constitution's Thirteenth Amendment ended slavery. But blacks saw little improvement as freed people. Racist violence against black people was common. Local rules called "Black Codes" took away rights from black people. Black Codes kept blacks from owning property, traveling freely, and holding many jobs. Eventually Southern states passed racist laws. These laws kept blacks separate from whites in education, work, and public places.

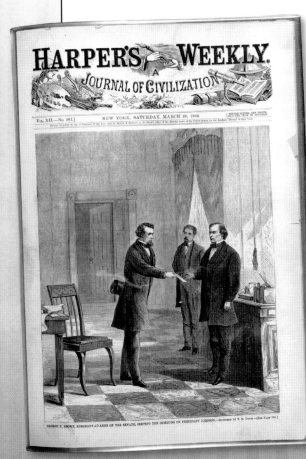

Andrew Johnson became the first sitting U.S. president to be impeached on February 24, 1868.

Many Northern leaders still had power after the war, both in government and in the military. Ulysses S. Grant was elected president in 1868 and served two terms. Grant was an honest president but a poor judge of people. He was surrounded by corruption, and his administration was one of the most corrupt in American history.

William Sherman replaced Grant as commander in chief of the army and served for 14 years. He was replaced as commander in chief in 1884 by Philip Sheridan. George McClellan was elected governor of New Jersey in 1877.

Edwin Stanton remained secretary of war, but resigned when President Johnson's impeachment trial ended without a conviction. President Grant later appointed him to the Supreme Court, but Stanton died four days later. William Seward stayed on under Johnson as secretary of state. In 1867 he helped buy Alaska from Russia.

The American public thought Seward's purchase of Alaska was a waste of money. Many jokingly referred to the future 49th state as "Seward's Folly" and "Seward's Icebox."

Grant was first inaugurated president on March 4, 1869. A major focus of his administration was rebuilding the South and protecting freed slaves.

After their defeat, Southern leaders faced more hardships than Northern leaders. Jefferson Davis was released from prison after two years and was never put on trial for treason. He retired to his Mississippi home where he wrote *The Rise and Fall of the Confederate Government.* Alexander Stephens was elected to Congress from Georgia in 1866. But Congress, dominated by Northern Republicans, refused to seat Stephens. He was elected again to Congress in 1872 and allowed to serve this time, which he did for 10 years. Robert E. Lee became president of Washington College in Lexington, Virginia. He served there for the last five years of his life. After his death the college was renamed Washington and Lee University in his honor.

After his arrest, Davis was imprisoned at Fort Monroe in Virginia. Initially he was a suspect in President Lincoln's assassination.

Southern cities such as Richmond, Virginia, were in ruins after the war. Repairing physical damage was one goal of the Reconstruction period (1865–1877).

Great leaders took the United States into the terrible Civil War and great leaders reunited the nation afterward. After the war the power of the federal government grew stronger. Within a few decades the United States became the world power it remains today.

GLOSSARY

abolitionist (ab-uh-LI-shuhn-ist)—a person who called for the immediate end of slavery before the Civil War

amputate (AM-pyuh-tayt)—to cut off someone's arm, leg, or other body part, usually because the part is damaged

arsenal (AR-suh-nuhl)—a place where weapons are stored

delegation (de-li-GAY-shuhn)—a group that speaks for a country

economy (i-KAH-nuh-mee)—the ways in which a country handles its money and resources

graft (GRAFT)—illegal practice such as bribery used to secure gains in politics or business

impeach (im-PEECH)—to bring formal charges against a public official who may have committed a crime while in office

inaugurate (in-AW-gyuh-rate)—to swear an official into public office with a formal ceremony

parole (pah-ROLL)—release from prison after serving less than the original sentence

plantation (plan-TAY-shuhn)—a large farm found in warm areas; before the Civil War, plantations in the South used slave labor

quartermaster (KWOR-tur-MASS-tur)—military department or officer in charge of getting supplies to troops

secede (si-SEED)—to formally withdraw from a group or an organization, often to form another organization

siege (SEEJ)—an attack on a castle, fort, or other enclosed location; a siege is usually meant to force the people inside the enclosed location to give up

READ MORE

Bader, Bonnie. *Who Was Robert E. Lee?* New York: Grosset & Dunlap, an imprint of Penguin, 2014.

Collins, Terry. *Robert E. Lee: The Story of the Great Confederate General.* American Graphic. Mankato, Minn.: Capstone Press, 2011.

Wittman, Susan S. *Heroes of the Civil War.* The Story of the Civil War. North Mankato, Minn.: Capstone Press, 2015.

CRITICAL THINKING USING THE COMMON CORE

1. Why did slavery disappear in the North but continue in the South in the 1800s? (Key Ideas and Details)

2. What actions did President Lincoln take that showed him to be an effective wartime leader? Use information from the book and other sources to support your answers. (Integration of Knowledge and Ideas)

3. How did Jefferson Davis and Alexander Stephens differ in their attitudes toward the Confederacy and the war? Use other sources to support your answer. (Craft and Structure)

4. What qualities did Grant have that made him a more effective commander in chief than McClellan? Use specific events and incidents from the book to support your answer. (Integration of Knowledge and Ideas)

5. In what ways did racism and political fighting continue in the postwar period? Use information from the book and other sources to support your answers. (Key Ideas and Details)

INTERNET SITES

FactHound offers a safe, fun way to find Internet sites related to this book. All of the sites on FactHound have been researched by our staff.

Here's all you do:

Visit *www.facthound.com*

Type in this code: 9781491420089

INDEX